Walking Brian Home

One Young Man's Story of Faith in the Face of Death

Alice Jane Stuckey

ISBN 978-1-64458-299-2 (paperback)
ISBN 978-1-64458-300-5 (digital)

Christian Faith Publishing, Inc.
832 Park Avenue
Meadville, PA 16335
www.christianfaithpublishing.com

Printed in the United States of America

One year ago, Brian took a turn for the worse, and he began his last leg of his journey home.

In all reality, Brian's road trip began with the mother's prayers. Even before his mother and father knew he existed, the creator of the universe was at work.

"You knit me together in my mother's womb" (Psalm 139:13). I can't imagine any mother wanting a child more than I wanted Brian. I loved my nieces, but like Hannah of old, I prayed for a child of my own.

"I prayed for this child and the Lord has given me what I asked for" (1 Samuel 1:27).

I was going to be the mother that Grandma had been Grandma to me. He would know that he was loved unconditionally. He was going to be nurtured, and trained, and encouraged to be his best. We would work together and play together. We would learn together, and we would pray together.

God answered that prayer in the wee hours of the night of September 12, 1971. Brian Keith Stuckey arrived two months early, weighing only 4 pounds and 11 ounces.

Brian Infant

Foolishly, two weeks earlier, I had been putting a roof on a barn with my father-in-law, encouraging an early entry into an anything but normal, mundane life.

I carried that baby with me from the sink, to the fields, and to the chair where I studied Scripture. We traveled to the laundromat and to the store together. Just as when I carried him inside of me, we danced around the house and sang sweet songs to Jesus.

Being premature meant he had to stay in the hospital for three weeks until his weight grew to five pounds.

I made a commitment to Jesus back in January of 1967 when I put him on in baptism, and no man or child was going to keep me from fulfilling it. So, his very first Sunday home, Brian was in church with me.

Deciding I was going to teach Brian about Jesus when he was eighteen months old, I offered to start a class at church for the four little ones his age.

Brian was a Polly parrot and a bit of a showoff from early on. Reciting his ABCs and counting in Spanish at the age of two and three and reciting the books of the old and new Testaments to the table over from us in a restaurant became the norm.

You can only imagine how dismayed and agonized I was when a voice at the other end of the line said, "We need to have Brian tested four LD (learning disability) classes, because he cannot hop, or skip, or catch a ball."

Up until this time, I believed he knew everything. Never again would I entrust my son's education solely to the school system. Testing actually showed Brian to be on the top of the ninth level of Stanford-Binet scale.

We tried for two and a half years to make LD classes work for him but to no avail.

"I'm in the dummy class." he would tell me.

Once, after pulling Brian out of the public school and putting him into a private school, a former teacher told me that "Brian was too well-behaved. To get along in school, you have to be a punk."

Brian thrived and blossomed at St. Mary's. His best friend had skipped a grade, and they could talk on the same intellectual level.

Brian took his smiling, loving attitude to school with him. He adjusted well to the larger classes and amazed everyone with his Bible knowledge.

"Sit down," the class would reprimand. "You already got an A."

Brian never missed a day in high school. He loved his teachers and his classmates. As fate would have it, when he ran for class office with three other boys against four girls, he was the only one of the boys elected.

Brian was a shy boy and never dated in high school.

"Now that I am a class officer," he said, "I guess I will have to find someone to go to the homecoming and the prom with."

He did, but first the girls had to meet twenty qualifications. They could not smoke or drink. They had to be a Christian and the topper was, they had to realize this was not a date but just an escort.

Even though Brian was in National Honor Society, he opted not to go to college. He passed his real estate test at seventeen and waited until he could be licensed at eighteen. His youth, however, was detrimental to his career.

Brian had been helping with his dad who was in a full-blown manic and PTSD episode in 1994. Little did Brian know when he drove a VA patient to the bus station, the path he was on would take a sharp turn to the mall and a short-term key holder position at Walden's Book Store.

What an excellent choice for a young man who loved learning— be it history, Bible, *Dungeons and Dragons*, or any number of subjects.

It was here that Brian made many lasting friends. Many of the gamers became part of his group of role players. I, myself, have never experienced such a group of loyal friends as these were. They were like a royal knighthood.

God has a way of placing us where he wants us. A man from church offered to give him a hundred dollars a month to go to college and leave his mother's apron strings. Brian said yes only to prove the man wrong and chose, OVC (Ohio Valley College). He majored in Bible and minored in Family Ministry and Counseling. Brian had been working with the teens at church since he graduated and felt this would aid him in his love of teaching God's word.

1997 Brian Trench Coat College

Once more, the friends Brian made during this time became family, disproving that blood is thicker than water.

Even with a 4.0 GPA, college days ended after only three semesters.

I was working in the pharmacy and could not keep an eye on his dad. My husband was threatening to shoot the tires out of the zoning trustees' cars. Brian, my knight in shining armor, as was his style, came home to rescue this damsel in distress, his mother.

So it came to be father and son working in the Stuckey Agency, side by side; working in the Stuckey fields, side by side.

In January of 1999, I left the pharmacy to walk alongside of my husband and my son. With computer rapidly becoming the way of business, Bill needed both of us to help him run his insurance business.

In 2004, Brian became our second agent. He was a fast learner and quite the personable businessman. As with his bookstore job and college, he never saw those who walked through the door of the agency as clients. He saw them as friends and had genuine concern for their joys and struggles.

Brian had become acquainted with a pretty, young lady from Case Western, who was studying to be a doctor.

Both Brian and Michele were to be attendants in a friend's wedding in 2007. Since Brian knew how much she liked to swing dance, the Christmas before the wedding, Brian thought he would take a lesson or two. That lesson turned into six years of lesson. He fell in love with dance. He lived it and breathed it. He danced it and talked it and even taught it.

Brian was responsible for organizing the first chapter of USA Dance in Sandusky and was its first president. "Someday," he thought, "I will own a dance studio."

Brian and his Girlfriend, Cindy, Dancing the Cha Cha
to Ayiesha Woods, "You Make Me Happy." song

7

In the summer of 2011, Brian noticed he was having a problem doing his spinning hat trick. He thought he was out of practice. Then he noticed he had a problem controlling the mouse when he was using his computer. He mentioned it to his doctor at his annual checkup. The doctor said to keep an eye on it, but he didn't think it was anything.

In the fall, Brian's hand was no better, so he made an appointment to have it checked out.

One doctor and another and still more. One test, one guess and another. No one knew.

In November of 2011, he got the answer I had feared, but Brian never expected.

I waited in the waiting room while Brian had another EMG. It wasn't long until the nurse came out with him. She gave him a hug and wished him luck.

"Mom," Brian said, as we walked down the hall together, "the doctor says I have ALS, and there is no cure for it. I know where I am going, and I know you know where I am going, but I am sad for Daddy and Cindy."

Daddy was an atheist. Cindy was a girlfriend he had met while he taught dance to Christian music at church.

It seems when the doctor gave him his diagnosis, he walked out of the room and left him alone with the nurse.

We talked heart-to-heart, mother to son, son to mother, believer to believer, all the way home. What did this all mean? What did God have in store for him?

We remembered how Satan had said Job only obeyed God because God gave him everything. Satan asked to take away from Job and see how he would turn on God. But God knew Job's heart. He knew Job could be trusted to be faithful to the end. And he was. He would not follow his wife's advice. "Curse God and die."

God also knew the same was true of Brian. He would be faithful to the end.

Being faithful does not mean sitting by and doing nothing.

My once dexterous, staff-twirling, dancing knight soon found himself on the ground. He used to bound down stairs from the upper office to the agency below or dance to the silent music going on in his head while he talked to the office girls. How his feet moved in worship as he whispered, "This is a rumba, Mom." But now it took all his effort not to trip and fall.

His speech became slurred, and he sounded drunk when he answered the office phone.

Finally, in April of 2012, the first diagnosis of ALS was confirmed by the Cleveland Clinic.

He did not want to believe it. He went the University Hospital, hoping for a diagnosis of Lyme disease. He was told it could be both. There was no cure for ALS, so he sought out a Lyme doctor in Pennsylvania. He made the monthly trip for the next ten months.

He continued to do his youth ministry, to help his dad—crawling on his hands and knees around the field to take the electric fence down. He took dance lessons and danced at parties. We would hear a thump and see Brian picking himself up off the floor to dance again with Cindy.

If you would have told me a year before Brian's symptoms began, nine months before that I would be watching my only child walking the road of certain death in three to five years, I would have first thought, "No way." Or, "Is he going to be killed in a car wreck?" But Lou Gehrig's? No way. I've only known one person to suffer from ALS and that person was a member of our church. I had not known him personally.

I had no clue what an agonizing wait we would have when shortly after Bria's fortieth birthday, we discovered his writing had become illegible, and his hand had stayed bent in the form of his computer mouse.

We joked about his turning forty and falling apart. He was angry that the computer use in our insurance agency may have caused carpel tunnel, and he may require surgery.

Up to this point, other than allergies, Brian had been a specimen of perfect health. He passed for a man much younger than his years.

Other than the time spent with his time dancing and enjoying the new steps he was learning, Brian volunteered for junior and senior high groups at the chapel and kept up on the weird, wired world of the teens.

Ever since school days, he would get together with his buddies to play strategy games, whenever the group was free.

He also kept busy helping his dad with the many projects on the family homestead. He plowed and planted the fields, cleaned the chicken coop, poured concrete, cut brick, and laid block for the buildings they were constructing. They cut grass and put it in the mulcher. Brian lived on a three-hundred-foot hill, and when the path was too wet for the tractor, he would push the wheelbarrow full up. There was no physical feat he could not accomplish.

I remember thinking as I sat alone at the table with my husband, Bill, Christmas day of 2011 about Tom and his experience with ALS. "Is this how it will be next year at Christmas? Will I be all alone? Will Brian have gone home to God?"

Brian was my only child. I didn't get pregnant right away after marriage. I thought that God was punishing me for the sex abuse of my childhood. Brian only weighed four pounds eleven ounces when he was born and four pounds three ounces when I first held him. I had foolishly been putting a barn roof on when I was six-and-a-half months along. I dropped the rafters, and he also dropped. He came at seven months.

I adored my little baby. He sat in his swing while I worked around the house. He sat in his carrier seat in the drawer beside the sink while I did the dishes. I sang as I danced with him in my arms singing, "Let me call you sweetheart. I'm in love with you. Let me hear you tell me that you love me too. Put your arms around me, baby hold me tight. And me and Brian Stuckey, will dance all through the night."

"You couldn't handle, Dad," he protested whenever he thought about of leaving home. Brian had become my protector after Bill's first bad episode with PTSD and bipolar. He was my knight in shining armor.

"Don't worry Brian," I would tell him. "God will take care of me."

Little did I know how I was prophesizing my future. I knew he had been with me through the years and tears of my life. But never before did I feel so helpless.

"So, are you going to ask Cindy to marry you, now?" I inquired that day, on our way home from being told of his terrible disease.

"I don't want to make her a widow, Mom. She's had so much bad luck with men."

"You need to give her a choice. You should not make that decision for her."

"I'll have to decide who I'll give my swords and books to," he stated calmly. "And where will I be buried, Mom?"

"You need to wait and see what Cindy says," I calmly sat there.

"I'll have to tell Dad right away when we get home."

I entered the office and asked Bill to take the apples in for me. Brian waited for him. Then when Bill had left, I turned toward the girls and blurted out, "He has Lou Gehrig's."

Cheryl dropped the phone and asked if she could call them back. Becky and Cheryl hugged me, and I cried. I told them it would be okay. He loved Jesus.

"God is good in the good times and He is good in the bad times."

It was a bittersweet time. ALS is nearly fatal in three to five years. Bummer. It was sweet that Brian had admitted to being in love with his dance partner. It was awesome to know that God was going to use Brian in unthinkable ways that I could only dream for the furthering of His kingdom.

I tried to get the word out to his many friends, so they could start praying for and encouraging him. Emails, Facebook, and phone calls. People who told their friends, churches, and families were all praying for Brian.

The show of support was unreal. So many folks truly cared about Brian. Dancers, gamers, church family, relatives, former classmates, and even insureds. I had never seen so much support in my life. God is so good! He brought us an amazing rainbow of friends.

Jerri, the mother of a classmate who had passed from a heart attack, stopped in at our agency with tears in her eyes. Jerri had worked at the grade school where Brian and Christie went. She brought Brian a lap prayer cloth the altar Rosary had made and prayed over.

I phoned Sue, the director of Erie county's Serving Our Seniors. I had met Sue in 1994 through a Christian caregivers' support group after Bill was diagnosed with Mixed Mania and PTSD from Vietnam. Brian had become close to Sue when USA Dance had a benefit for Serving Our Seniors a few years earlier. As president of the club, Brian and his vice-president, Russ, had organized the Dancing with the North Coast Stars to earn money for insulin for the elderly who could not afford it.

Sue called the newspaper to tell them what had happened to our son. In two days' time, the *Register* was out interviewing Brian, his dad, and me.

Man fights for his life

By ANNIE ZELM
zelm@sanduskyregister.com

NORWALK

Brian Stuckey has trained himself to think on his feet.

As he quicksteps in a snappy suit and fedora, he's always envisioning the next sequence.

When he goes to battle with his fellow warriors in a strategy game, he's plotting a few steps ahead of his opponent.

And as an insurance agent, he's constantly reminding others to be prepared.

But these days, Brian is a man whose next steps couldn't be more uncertain.

Sometimes, just putting one foot in front of the other is taxing.

He's lost muscle in his right leg, causing him to stumble frequently. The rolling hills on his parent's Milan Township farm are especially tricky.

He takes more breaks when he's dancing.

It's hard to make long-term plans when he doesn't know if he'll be alive two years from now, much less walking.

He'd like to plan a future with his girlfriend and dance partner, Cindy Haycook, but illness has brought difficult discussions to the forefront.

■ See STUCKEY, Page A5

Register photo/ANGELA WILHELM

Brian Stuckey, who doctors say is showing symptoms of ALS, also known as Lou Gehrig's Disease, in his office Thursday at Stuckey Agency in Norwalk.

Brian Shares his Faith in the Sandusky Register

Brian Stuckey in his office Thursday at Stuckey Agency in Norwalk. Doctors say Stuckey is showing signs of ALS, also known as Lou Gehrig's Disease.

STUCKEY

■ FROM PAGE A1

At some point, everything he's done without thought — swallowing, speaking, even breathing — may be nearly impossible to do on his own.

Puzzling prognosis

In November 2010, Brian noticed an odd quirk while rehearsing his routine for a ballroom dancing showcase. His trademark move was tossing his fedora and catching it with a quick curl of his index finger.

No matter how hard he tried, he couldn't seem to do it anymore.

He couldn't coax his thumb to straighten into a thumbs-up, or pick up a pen without dropping it.

He assumed it was carpal tunnel syndrome, and he didn't give it much thought, in fact, until about a year later.

Last November, doctors told him he appeared to have symptoms of amyotrophic lateral sclerosis, or ALS, also known as Lou Gehrig's disease.

The disease wages war on the nerve cells in the brain and spinal cord, interfering with signals sent to the muscles. Eventually, the body shuts down as the muscles weaken. The cause is unknown, and there is no cure.

Many patients die slowly and painfully within three to five years of diagnosis, according to the U.S. Library of Medicine.

For Brian, perhaps the only strand of hope is that he hasn't been given an official diagnosis.

His symptoms seem to be improving with therapy, which isn't typical for people with the degenerative disease. At 40 years old, he's at least 10 years younger than the average age of most ALS patients when they start experiencing symptoms.

Next month, he's headed to the Cleveland Clinic for a second opinion.

Dance for a cause

■ **WHAT:** A live Big Band show, featuring Swing City Big Band and a potluck table
■ **When:** 7:10 p.m. April 28. Doors open at 6:30 p.m.
■ **Where:** Elk's Grand Ballroom, 120 E. Adams St., Sandusky
■ **Cost:** $20. All tickets sold in advance due to limited space. Proceeds benefit Brian Stuckey. To reserve tickets call 419-626-2910.

Acceptance

While he hopes doctors discover the culprit is some other illness that mimics ALS — late-stage Lyme Disease, he's learned, has similar symptoms but is treatable — Brian is already preparing to face death.

A volunteer youth leader at The Chapel, he finds himself frequently turning to the book of Job, someone who used suffering to glorify God rather than curse him.

He said he doesn't like to think about the way his life may eventually end, but that painful time, compared to eternity, is "like having a 24-hour flu compared to the rest of your life."

"I'm not afraid to die," Brian said. "I don't like leaving my father or mother and Cindy, and I don't like seeing them hurt.

"But dying for me is not a bad thing. I believe in heaven. I'm going to live as long as I can. I'm going to dance as long as I can, I'm going to minister as long as I can, I'm going to get together with my friends as long as I can to do strategy games. I'm going to help on the farm as long as I can."

Brian considers himself lucky to have so much support from his family, church, gaming friends and fellow dancers.

His parents, Alice and Bill Stuckey,

started the insurance agency at their home when their son was only 4 years old. They welcomed him into the family business after he graduated college.

Brian's mother has fleeting thoughts of what life could be like a year or two from now, when she and Bill may find themselves celebrating the holidays alone or working side by side in their office without their son handling claims nearby.

In those moments, she cries.

Mostly, though, her son inspires her.

"It's bittersweet to see what God is doing and to know that God has such a faith in Brian," she said. "He has to, because God never gives you more than you can handle."

Bill is more pragmatic, focusing on experimental treatments by the Israeli-based research firm known as Brain-Storm. He's encouraged by a recent clinical trial that showed patients treated with stem cells had improved swallowing, breathing and muscle function.

Longtime friend Timothy Nyman, who owns the Black Tie Dance Studio with his wife Artemisia, said Brian is one of the most selfless and hardworking people he's ever known.

"He's the guy that you think, if anybody was to get something like this, why him?" he said.

At times, Brian finds himself asking why.

But he also thinks, "Why not me?"

"I wouldn't want this to go on anybody else," he said. "I wouldn't want somebody else to suffer. I hope it's not ALS, but if it is, I hope that I'll be able to be an example to people ... that people will see my devotion to God, both in life and even in the way I die.

Said Brian: "There's a quote I try to live by: 'When you were born, you cried and the world rejoiced. Live your life in such a way that when you die, the world cries and you rejoice.'"

The *Norwalk Reflector* got word of the *Register* article and wanted to do a story of their own.

Ailing St. Paul graduate dances as long as he can

ALS

Continued from Pg. A-1

He lost about half the strength in his right hand and can't straighten its pointer finger.

By AARON KRAUSE
Reflector Staff Writer
akrause@norwalkreflector.com

Stuckey

Brian Stuckey loves to partner with ladies for ballroom dancing.

When a lady lacks a partner at a social, he'll serve in that role for her; he wants her to feel special, rather than left out.

And he's not married, so it's no big deal.

The 1989 St. Paul graduate, 40, wants to continue partnering for as long as he can.

His partner, though, may need to catch him if he falls from exhaustion or inability to maintain his balance.

That is likely to continue happening: A doctor believes Stuckey has amyotrophic lateral sclerosis (ALS), aka Lou Gehrig's Disease.

There is no cure for the disease and it is always fatal. Many patients die slowly and painfully within three to five years of diagnosis, according to the U.S. Library of Medicine.

The doctor doesn't know for sure, because Stuckey's symptoms have improved with therapy — which is unusual for people with the disease. So

Sandusky and Norwalk. He works with teenagers at the Sandusky location and with junior high students in Norwalk. Stuckey also conducts Bible study on Thursday nights.

Stuckey said everyone in his church community, dancing community and his work community, has supported him. He's also received support from fellow high school graduates.

"I've had wonderful amounts of support from everyone in my life," Stuckey said. "It's been amazing."

Stuckey, an insurance agent, first realized something was wrong while dancing. He first took lessons so a friend would have a partner at a wedding they both attended. Over time, he learned a trick in which he spins his top hat off his head and catches it with his last finger.

All of a sudden, he could no longer catch it with his finger.

Stuckey thought he had Carpal Tunnel syndrome.

Within a few months, Stuckey had trouble legibly writing his name.

A doctor ruled out Carpal Tunnel.

Stuckey will seek a second opinion at the Cleveland Clinic on April 11. He said he's been told he might have other conditions that are treatable.

Regardless of the final diagnosis, Stuckey said he's not afraid of dying. He said there is a life after this one.

"I think heaven's going to be great," he said.

"He is so full of faith," said his mother, Alice. "Everything he does he wants to do for God's glory. Jesus is an everyday word in our conversation."

It extends to his volunteer work as a youth leader for The Chapel in

See ALS / Pg. A-6

His speech also became slurred, he walks with a limp and cannot dance for long periods of time before taking a break.

Although a doctor in Lorain told Stuckey there's a high probability he has ALS, "it's giving me some hope that I might have something other than ALS," he said.

Stuckey is the only child of Alice and Bill Stuckey.

Alice Stuckey said she always tells him she and her husband only had one because they got the best first.

She said it hurts her to see her son lose many of his physical abilities.

But she's relying on her faith to keep her strong.

"I know God's going to be with us through all of this," she said. "I really believe I am strong enough to handle this with Christ's strength — not with my own, but through Christ."

Meanwhile, Stuckey will continue partnering with ladies for dances for as long as he's able.

Brian's Story Appears in the Norwalk Reflector

I knew the way they interviewed him that this article would not mention anything about God. I was definitely wrong! That article, also, witnessed to Brian's faith.

Brian continued to do his daily office work. He plowed and disk the fields. He helped his father cut down trees.

It was a bright sunny day when our friend, CJ, drove us with our niece as a copilot, to Cleveland Clinic to see Dr. Pioio, the head of the ALS department.

The male nurse was extremely nice, and the doctor was friendly. He took his time talking to us and allowing us to ask questions. He had Brian walk toe-to-toe and check his reflexes and on and on. We asked about Lyme Disease. We live near the woods with many deer. He didn't think so, but he would do blood work for that, also, when he did the other blood work. He was testing for copper poison. He told us there was a slim chance, "Very slim. Less than one percent," that could have something coming from outside the body causing the muscle deterioration. In other words, Brian had Lou Gehrig's disease.

Besides the seven vials of blood they took from him, they did another MRI at the Avon Clinic.

The clinic was booked up until the end of July or the beginning of August. That would be a three– or four-month wait.

A lady from *Norwalk*, wrote to him about Lyme disease. Now, he became really confused. What should he do? Go to Pennsylvania to a doctor to have that checked out? Was it just another wild goose chase? He kept in touch with his friend who was an immunology PhD and was going into an MD residency. She thought the Lyme doctor was just out to get money. Brian emailed Dr. Preston. He said Lyme is a fad right now.

Should Brian get assistance through a breathing mechanism? Should he use a feeding tube to help him live longer? He wondered.

When I told him his dad and I would care for him, he told me I was already sixty-two and Dad was sixty-seven. We wouldn't be able to help that long. He had no children of his own, no brothers or sisters. He would end up a vegetable with a brain in a nursing home.

I hated to hear him talk that way, but I couldn't tell him how to feel or think. I had to respect his wishes.

He knew scripture frontwards and backwards. He knew heaven was waiting for him, but he didn't like the process of getting there.

He was angry with God. He didn't think God was fair. He had allowed Cindy and Brian to get close. God was cruel to Cindy. Why now?

I knew it was his grief and anger and depression. I tried not to preach to him. I prayed for him and Cindy. I asked God to fill me with his strength. I couldn't do it on my own. I tried to tell people God was good all the time. To say how much faith God must have in him. To remind them of Job.

It was all so unreal. Brian was still walking and talking and dancing and plowing. Sure, he tired more easily. Instead of dancing three hours straight, he was lucky to dance three dances straight.

Brian had reconnected with Russel, who was a college friend that ended up in a prison in Tennessee. He loved Russell and believed him innocent. I also loved Russell. Though he could not come and support Brian in person, he did write and encourage Brian.

> Dear Brian,
> I feel like I should have done this sooner… your mother has been telling me about your recent medical crisis. My heart goes out to you like you wouldn't believe. I can empathize with the horror and helplessness of facing the possibility of losing so much you love due to circumstances out of your control.
> What words of comfort can I offer? I remember so well how you described your life and how much you enjoy it. And none of us ever knows why God puts such challenges in our life. I'm sure you have prayed in your own way for deliverance and comfort and you can depend on me to add my own prayers.
> My friend, I pray that I can give you some strength to face this. I, myself, find my own situation difficult to handle and it is only a small thing compared to yours.

If I could wish anything for you, it would be that you get a miracle either in healing or in realizing God's purpose in this. Maybe that sounds a bit too much, but I would not wish on anyone the fear of uncertainty.

Then again, maybe you are stronger than I'm assuming, and I hope I haven't just insulted you or any peace you have attained.

Your friend, Russell

January 26, 2012

Dear Russell

I must begin by saying that I am sorry that I have not written sooner. Please know that despite my lack of written correspondence, you have been in my thoughts and prayer nearly constantly since I last wrote. My mother has kept me up-to-date with the happenings in your life as each letter arrived, and I must tell you that I was grieved to hear the result of your trial. It is my prayer that the judge shows mercy in the sentencing.

Concerning my neurological problem, although I have my moments of frustration, my overall attitude is trusting in God and His providence over this situation. Although I would love to have my body restored to its former health, I have a great desire for God to use my affliction to reach those that my life touches who do not know Him. If I had to choose between the restoration of my health and the restoration of someone's relationship with God, I'd choose their situation every time.

This said, I am very glad for the support that you and many of my friends in this area offer me. If my count is correct, I may have as many as 1,500 people consistently bringing my condition before the Lord in prayer. Although many of these people attend church in the area, some who I never knew had a relationship with God have called me to express their concern and their desire to pray for me.

It is encouraging to see that the physical therapy that I am undergoing seems to be helping some. Before I started, I could not touch my little finger of my right hand to my right thumb, nor could I start my car without leaning forward in my seat... now I can do both.

I am very happy to say that I can also still dance, though now, I have to take more breaks instead of dancing for hours on end. Many of my friends tell me that I'm just being brought down to their level rather than "Superman." The problem is, of course, I'm used to being more than average when it comes to my strength, dexterity, and endurance.

I think the situation is hardest on my dance partner, Cindy. I have no doubt that Cindy loves me with all her heart, and I know that it is hard for her to see when I struggle with my frustrations. I try to maintain my honor as I deal with this for both Cindy's sake and my own. I've told myself repeatedly that I have lived a life of honor and courage for forty years, and I've not about to be fearful now. Still, I know Cindy has enough unspoken fears for the both of us.

With Love and Respect!

Your Friend,
Brian Stuckey

March 10, 2012

Dear Russell,

First of all, I want you to know how special you are to Brian and myself. I pray God will show you purpose in your situation and you can bring glory to Him.

I am reminded of so many promises of God and of his never-ending goodness, especially now.

Wednesday, the 7th, Brian had an EMG on his arm. As we were walking down the hall to leave, he told me, "The doctor says I have Lou Gehrig's." Do you know what that is? ALS?

He could live three years, five years, or even ten years if he is lucky. But he will lose all mobility and his speech but will keep his mind to the end. Then at last, he will suffocate into the Lord's arms.

He says he is ready to go. He will be happy cause he knows where he is going. But he is sad for his dad and Cindy. He knows Bill is an unbeliever and Cindy loves him so much. It hurts to see him cry—to see him choke when he swallows, to see him weak as he dances. To see him fall down and to misunderstand his words as he talks to me. But I know God will use him to do magnificent things for His kingdom and glory.

In fact, I have already seen good come from this horrible disease.

It is bittersweet. He is a bright light to so many so love him. He is scared of going through the process.

So many believers and non-believers have told him, if anyone deserves prayer, it is him. A pastor at First Christian has asked him if he feels up to it to speak for his congregation.

I asked Brian if he was going to ask Cindy to marry him now and he said he didn't want to make her a widow. Cindy has accepted his proposal. I don't know when or how it will be or where they will live. But I did tell Brian it would give him peace of mind to know we would have Cindy to care for us when he is gone.

Yes, we pray for a miracle, but we trust in the Lord.

John 16:33, Jesus tells us, "In this world you will have troubles," but He has overcome the world!

I want you to hold on to these thoughts, too. And to know you are my spiritual son and you remain in my prayers and in the prayers of many of my friends.

Though Brian's friend, Eric Lapata, was away in Michigan at preacher's school, they kept in touch through email.

On Apr 12, 2012, at 11:56 p.m., Brian Stuckey wrote:

Hello Eric,

Concerning my bad news, I'm fine with it. I have already had the opportunity to publicly proclaim my trust in God in two front page articles... since I believe Satan is targeting me... if he wants to escalate this, then he'd best be ready for the consequences. I'll find every opportunity to be an example of trust in God and seek every door God opens to publicly sing God praises, even if that means programing my testimony into a computer so I can present it with my own voice once my voice is gone. If Satan wants a fight, let him come. I know my damage to his plans will pale in comparison to Jesus's sacrifice, as it should and must, but if my health problems can in any way mirror Satan's loss to our Lord and Savior, then I will happily die with a smile on my face. I'd love to lead as many souls to Jesus as I can before I die.

Don't think that I lack moments of sadness, for I'd be a liar if I said anything contrary. These are especially due to having to see the hurt and pain this is causing Cindy. If I have one thing I don't understand, it's why God allowed us to get close if this would hurt her so. I hate to say it, but it almost seems cruel to my mind especially given her past history of failed marriages. Doesn't she deserve some happiness in her life. It's probably the only part of this that I struggle not to hold against God.

At present, I've chosen to withhold the news of my probable diagnosis with ALS from Cindy until it is official. I want to see her smile a little while longer, and I fear the of an ALS diagnosis might send her into a deep depression and I might not see a genuine smile again. I'm hoping to get her into counseling with Pastor Dave Brown, or Mark Seymore before I tell her.

Serving our Savior,
Brian

After Serving in the Youth Group, Brian and His
Good Friend, Eric Lapata Catch Up on Life

September 25, 2012

Russell, never ever think you are bothering us,
if we don't answer. Try back. I answered the one
night, but it didn't go through. It would help if
I had an idea what days or evenings you could
call and what time. Some Fridays, I go to watch
Brian dance and I don't get home until about ten
or so p.m. our time. Thursdays for another six
weeks, I will be gone from five until nine-thirty.

Sunday a.m. I go to church. If I know when you will be calling, I can pretty much pass on supper out, the dance or Bible Study...

And yes, our perception does change with age; luck? Random good? Or blessing—God's good, and I think we become more observant to God's presence in our situation. I think the church of Christ called it God's providence.

If you had not gone to OVC; if Brian had not waited until twenty-five to go to college, if, if, if, then I would not have met you and come to love and care about you. Cheryl and Becky would not know of you or prayed for you or have been influenced by your faith. (They both have, you know.) I could go on and on. I am so blessed by God to be able to call you "friend."

As for Brian, he is sick today with a virus. He never got out of bed. It seemed to hit him harder than other years, but he is so run down this year.

Don't get me wrong. He is doing well. The doctor only gave him thirty percent chance of getting better when we saw him July eleventh. To think an antibiotic could make such a difference. In three weeks, his speech and swallowing improved.

In eight weeks, his hand improved. His walk improved. No, he is not what you remember him. His left hand is still skeletal. He has severe foot drop, but he does walk better than he did. It will take a long time to build the ankle muscles up— maybe never. And to get the fine motor control in his hands will mean a lot of work. But Brian is determined to work hard and give God the glory. This mom is proud! The people who have been encouraged by watching him go thru this is phenomenal, just as those who you have touched, will never be the same. Thank you, Russell. You are an awesome example.

Brian's dance instructors used their eighth anniversary in business to go to a fund-raiser to get Brian a voice recorder iPad for when he could not talk in the future.

In all my life, I could not imagine so many friends coming together in so short a notice to honor Brian.

Our first guests were no surprise. My best friend of fifty-eight years and her mother and husband. Brian felt comfortable enough with her to share his disappointment in the doctors. He wanted a bit of hope to hang on to. He had none.

Friends from dance, friends from church, friends from school, friends from the agency. Friends everywhere and from everywhere. Brian was loved, and I was so thankful for the support—not the money—but the emotional support letting him know how much they cared.

Brian and Cindy performed their cha-cha, "You Make Me Happy," for what Brian said he believed would be their last time.

Still no word from the ALS specialist. Then one day, it came in the mail—a fifteen-page report and on page six, "Now that ALS is certain."

What kind of doctor was this that just sent a report to tell his patient that he had Lou Gehrig's, and he would lose all his muscles, his voice, and eventually, die in two to five years?

Brian telephoned the clinic and asked for his doctor return his phone call. The nurse said she would tell him to call but to remember he was not the doctor's only patient.

The list results confused us. We didn't know much, but we did know the blood test results didn't make sense to us.

Waiting for the Cleveland Clinic to call wasn't an option for me. I phoned Brian's local doctor to see if he could order another Lyme test and told the nurse how Brian had been feeling. All the doctors were avoiding him. Even though Dr. Ruggle's nurse said he didn't understand the fifteen-page report from the clinic, he did order the Western blot test. It came back negative.

Brian decided to make an appointment with a Lyme doctor in Pennsylvania. He couldn't get in until July 11, 2012. The wait was long. The rules were strict, and the price was astronomical. But if he had Lyme, there was hope of a cure!

There were times Brian would wonder why now he had a girl-friend and a reason to live.

There were times he resolved himself to going home to heaven.

"If God didn't save Tom Stallings, why would he save him?" Brian was confused much of the time as to if it was really ALS or Lyme. Was he deluding himself?

Every time he prayed for direction, it seemed someone would email him, or call or approach him at church about how they had been crippled up and misdiagnosed. They went to the Lyme doctor in Pennsylvania or east of Cleveland, and now, they could walk again.

I printed off articles from the internet for Bill to read. Brian researched the diseases and our friend and secretary, Becky, researched also.

I began to believe Brian did not have ALS. He had Lyme or a virus.

The verse that said, "God who began a good work in you will see it to completion," ran through my head. I firmly believed God had more work for him to do. God had already allowed him to witness to many through the newspapers and his attitude. When God healed him, he would touch many more lives.

I read through my prayer journal.

January 2, 2012

Good Morning, thank you for being here with me and not a far off place.

January 18, 2012

Dear heavenly Father,

Life goes so fast this side of death. We are not guaranteed our next breath. Brian is so sure it is ALS now and he'll be dead in two years.

So now what? I need to do something. I can't just sit and watch him be discouraged. Pray? Yes, Lord. I can pray. Brian is in your hands. You know his heart, his fears, his hopes, his dreams, his health, and all. You are his creator, God.

March 10, 2012

Dear heavenly Father,

Thank you so much you would give your son for me. Now, please, let me love you so much to trust my son to you.

Lord, I know You have a big plan. I believe You have purposed Brian for something big, and You will not let him go home to you until it is accomplished.

It is bittersweet. Brian's prognosis is sad— heart wrenching. The thought of Brian marrying is joyous for both him and Cindy. A roller-coaster, but there is good as long as there is God.

March 12, 2012

Dear heavenly Father,

What a God you are! You are the one true God.

Thank you for loving me enough to grow me in you... to strengthen me in You, throughout the years, to prepare me for this time in my life. You've never failed me before, and You're not about to start failing me now! All glory and power be to Your name.

Father, thank You for your loving family. Thank you for the hope we have in You.

Lord especially be with my Brian. You can work a miracle. I know that! But, even if you chose not to, I know You will use all of this for Your glory. You have already started to. It's exciting to see how You turn sadness into good.

Praise and glory be to Your holy name. Amen.

March 22, 2012

Dear Father,

You are so high, so good, so mighty. You love me; You love Brian, and I know this. It is getting from knowing to trust.

I know you can do all things. I know now to trust you in Your mighty ways. I trust there is a heaven and hell, and Your son died for me and Brian and all peoples. I trust You said those who believe shall not perish. But this process is so much with Brian. It seems unreal. Lord, it happens to others, why not Brian?

March 31, 2012

Dear Lord,

Thank You for this day. God, you are my God, and I will praise and glorify Your name.

You always were. You always are, You always will be. Who better to trust in than You?

Lord, I was sad last night watching Brian dance. He looks like he is losing weight, but of course muscle weighs.

Lord, what Cindy told me about him not wanting to see the valleys with her, about made me want to cry. But Lord, I understand his legs are so weak.

Up and down like a wavy line—that is what Brian, Cindy, Bill, and I are feeling, Lord. I don't want you to let him die and take his hope. Lord, he is faithful to You. I want to ask why, but I know You will use this for your glory.

April 14, 2012

Dear Lord,

Today is the day Brian accepted You and was baptized in 1985 (twenty-six years ago). Lord, he has lived for You. Thank You for giving me a son who loves You even when he is upset because of allowing this to happen after he got so close to Cindy.

Lord, it is hard to believe Brian could be crippled in a year or so. It is sad. So why can't I cry? Help me to be a good mom to him. Let me be a faithful servant to You.

May 2, 2012

Dear Father,

You are the one who keeps me strong and who knows my future. I scarce believe Brian will be crippled and die. Not my Brian! But he is only mine because You loaned him to me. It thrills me to see the great things You are doing through him. But I admit to sadness to see him go through all of this. It makes me fearful of what lies ahead.

But I remember 2 Timothy 1:7, "But God has not given us a spirit of fear and timidity, but of power and love and self-discipline." I need to remember that.

June 21, 2012

I wander aimlessly from chore to chore—never really accomplishing the many tasks. They pile up to insurmountable, and I am overwhelmed.

My son is ill. I fear upsetting him. I just want him to feel loved. I get angry when people declare their love for him but are too busy to share their lives with him. He gives. They take.

That is the story of my friendships, too. I love to give and be kind.

July 1, 2012

Why not me?

Why was I born this time of history and in this culture? Why am I so blessed?

Why wasn't I born in a country filled with poverty and illness instead of in a country full of blessing, not only of food, shelter, and clothing, but of luxuries?

Why have I never experienced a devastating auto accident or fire? Why have I never been incarcerated?

> And now that Brian is ill and may be dying, I ask, why my son? Why not me? I am older. I've lived sixty-two years. What is it Lord that you want me to do? Why am I so blessed? What do you want me to do with the blessing of your storehouse? Show me your plans and purposes, O Lord.

We waited almost two months to see the Lyme literate doctor. We had to travel to Hermitage, Pennsylvania. I believed stronger than ever that it was a bacterial infection, or an autoimmune disease and that Brian was not going to die from this.

The doctor did not come out and say, "It's Lyme," but he did say he was going to start from scratch and sort things out himself. He told him to continue with his ALS doctor for now.

He prescribed 500 mg Biaxin in the morning for thirty days. He told him what vitamins to take and had him do a urine test on days three, five, and seven to FedEx out right away to be tested. He also told him to keep a journal because often, Lyme patients have foggy memories. So that, I also was keeping a journal of what I see going on with Brian.

July 12, 2012 Biaxin Day 1

> Depressed, irritable, disappointed, discouraged, pessimistic. He had like tunnel ears. His urine was cloudy. He was ready to put his things in order because he believed he'd be dead in two years. At first, the urine turned cloudy or gray. Then it cleared up.
>
> Days 2–3 were much the same as day one. Brian was very active entertaining a friend, dancing, walking a flea market, and busy until midnight both nights.
>
> About 4:00 a.m. on the fifth day, he got hot and cold and hot again. He felt queasy. He got

back to sleep about 5:15 a.m. and slept until 8:30 a.m.

He took a light nap for a few hours in the afternoon and felt okay.

Day 5 fever in the late afternoon, about five or six. Better appetite.

Day 7 or 8, he realized the pain and burning in his shoulders had subsided with only aches once in a while.

He became more irritated with his father, but I was not sure if that was because his dad was not paying attention or because of the reaction.

He lost his hope of getting better. He doubted if anyone would really know what he had.

By Friday, Brian realized his swallowing had improved and he wasn't choking.

Saturday, day 11 of his treatment, Brian had floaters in his urine. I believed it to be a definite sign that some bacteria were being killed in his system.

Low-grade fevers went on and then cold clamminess.

Brian used his braces only for times when he walked far or danced, and that was usually only the right leg.

Brian still drove, but often asked me to drive because he felt he had to be more cautious when he drove.

I am amazed how God encouraged us along our journey. So many people told us they were praying for us that I began to say, yeah, God has a busy signal and no one else could get through to Him, so He was going to have to heal Brian.

That God would allow us to have the honor of witnessing for Him, was truly amazing. Excitement grew in me each time someone mentioned Brian's faith. Brian was touching lives for Jesus. People were watching Brian face the unknown with a smile and courage that could only come from the almighty power of God.

How far reaching would the ripples of Brian's trust in God go?

At times, I asked God why. "Why Lord do we have so much encouragement from others? Why are so many folks concerned about Brian? Why are so many praying while others, who in their own struggles, were struggling, and seemed to be doing life and hardships alone? Was God trying to reach deep into my heart to motivate me to act on what I had noticed about these lonely hearts?

> Days 14 and 15, Brian had aches in his muscles like flu. Around 6:00 a.m., he got up feeling rough. He would feel warm to touch and then clammy. Then he would try to get comfortable. The temperature usually ranged from 97.6 to 98.7 or so.

Brian seemed to be feeling hopeless and just wondering which doctor was right. Was it Lyme? Was it ALS? Was it both or something else?

Brian later recalled what had happened during a praise service the chapel had three days after our first visit to the Lyme doctor.

We were worshiping and all of a sudden, he felt connected to God. He felt he heard a voice saying to him, "Brian, I will heal you!"

I didn't know of this until a few months later, when our friend, CJ, and I took Brian with us to McDonald's after one of his counseling appointments.

As he reviewed his session with Mark, he mentioned the praise night.

I made him stop and back up. "What are you talking about? You never told me."

He was afraid to say anything to anyone. He didn't know if it was real or if he was losing his mind. He was afraid he was hallucinating. He had only told three people about the incident—the wife of a woman whose husband passed of ALS, a co-youth leader, and his girlfriend.

Three weeks after he first went to the doctor in Pennsylvania, he prayed God would restore his voice, so he could be a more effective youth leader at church. It has been five months since he started slurring heavily. We would strain to make out what he was saying. It was frustrating both him and us.

Two days after he had prayed about his voice, he and his father sat in a restaurant together.

Brian ordered "Mello Yellow" and everyone looks at each other. Bill, Brian, and the waitress. They couldn't believe how clearly, he was speaking. Brian now had confirmation the voice at the praise night was real.

After this, Brian shared with me a conversation between him and his dad.

Bill had told Brian he was afraid to tell us, because he thought we'd laugh at him.

Bill, who has never in the forty-four years I've known him, acknowledged a power greater than himself. He has taken glory in being an atheist and being a self-made man.

Now, he told Brian he went down in the woods and talked to his trees. He told the trees, "I've always been good to you. I've only ever cut down dead trees, not you living ones. I only have one son. Can you give me a sign he is going to live?"

He then preceded to bring Brian's attention to a stump of a tree—a tree, which a friend had cut down before he died many years before. It had never shown any sign of life, but now, coming out of the rotting trunk was a green sprout.

I had to lean into God, if I was going to get through this and be the support to my son that I wanted to be. More prayers. More ups and downs.

November 5, 2012

I'm bummed today. I don't know why I feel so down. Or maybe I do. I am allowing my circumstances to dictate my mood. Bill isn't comprehending what I tell him.

And then there's Brian. He seems to be down cause he isn't getting better but at a plateau. Bill says he is getting better. I hate to say it, but I think he is walking worse, falling more, and slurring a lot, and is dopey with his hand. I hope I am imagining it all. Brian is talking to Bill about going on disability.

Everything right now seems so dark around me. And it is overwhelming. I can't imagine where I would be without my faith in Jesus.

December 8, 2012

Dear Russell,

I hope your holiday season is going okay and you are remembering the Savior coming to earth for your sins and mine. He is our only hope.

Speaking of hope, we heard from zoning yesterday in the mail, that we have another meeting this time the eleventh to build a ramp for Brian.

I pray it will pass this board, and we will be granted. Brian seems to be getting worse again. He got athlete's foot from swimming in the pool and therapy. His system is very run-down, and with the antibiotics he takes, the fungus has a good breeding ground. His therapist explained to me that when you have a neurological disorder and gets another ailment with it, your progress stops, and you regress. That is what is happening with Brian.

His speech has become really slurred again. His legs are weak and very unsteady. He falls often in the hallway, kitchen, by the tub, on the steps where he dances. It is so hard for him to turn over for me to apply the meds to his feet. And if he talks while he eats, he chokes and cannot catch his breath.

But I know, God is good, and His mercy endures forever. One of these days he will be whole again, if not here, then there.

January 16, 2013

Dear Father in heaven,

You are the great physician. You know how sad and down Brian is. I don't know if he has Lyme or ALS, but I know he is very depressed and unhappy. He thinks he'll be in a wheelchair by Easter. He said if he isn't better by his birthday, he's signing his car over to me. He told me to pray you'll take him home soon. Lord, if that is your plan, then I am fine with it, but I really want to see him get better. I know you have the power to raise Jesus. You have the power to cure Brian.

Lord, surround Brian with love. We need your encouragement.

February 5, 2013

Dear Lord,

Brian isn't sleeping at night. You know the reasons. Please help him to rest. It hurts to hear him say he is not a lion anymore. He is a weak old man. Lord, give me the words to show him his identity is in You and not his body.

My hope is in You, Lord.

February 15, 2013

Dear Father in heaven,

It blows my mind how you can be in heaven and here too. How you don't have an "open and closed" sign or a telephone off the hook.

March 7, 2013

Dear God,

That You are God, is obvious. The many miracles and working I see You do. Wow. I can't wait to get to haven and see how really active You were, and I didn't even know it.

You are the most amazing. Thank You. Thank You for the peace in my heart. I praise Your holy name. You are above all and in all.

Lord, be with my Brian, and Lord, help me to decide if I should or should not have Bible study and if so, what to study and when.

Brian and I used Facebook to share with others Brian's journey.

March 14, 2013, Norwalk, Ohio

I've been thinking, I want to share a little inspiration about Brian. I may have mentioned Brian does all kinds of exercises three to four hours a day. He has told me that when he does these, he offers them to God so that one day, he can be Jesus's hands and feet! Also, to strengthen his hands, he is printing out the Psalms and Proverb. (I guess than means he is getting spiritual exercise, also!) Praise God for Brian's positive outlook!

Brian's Last Tractor Ride

March 20, 2013

Dear Russell,

Words can't express how I love to receive your letters. You are quite an example of accepting the situation you are in and making the best of it. Thank you for showing me this side of you.

All of us who walk this earth have struggles. Some give up in defeat and helplessness. Others cling to their faith and trust in Christ to give them strength. My prayer is that God's strength will be very real to you and your wonderful attitude will continue. I love you, Russell.

When I was a girl, I wanted to have twenty boys; then I thought I wanted four boys; then a little girl. God gave me one son. But in His wisdom, has blessed me with many young men, and they call me mom and I call them "son." Brian's friends are my sons. Some are closer than others, but they are all my boys! You, dear, have always been in my heart since I met you way back in the OVC days.

I am not truly sure how Brian is doing. Maybe I am too close to judge his progress. Maybe I want too much too quickly. Patience. What a hard thing to practice. Trusting God when we cannot see the outcome. Life isn't easy, is it?

March 22, 2013

To Russell

I am glad you are able to learn from your experience. You and Brian are a lot alike. You could give up and just get by, but both of you make the best of a situation. It is that perseverance that I love. You are very strong. I am so proud of you.

Brian talked to his former girlfriend, Michele. She is afraid by leaving the old pic line in that the new line may have been cross contaminated. Also, Michele was concerned about his speech and his exasperating. Joe notices his needing to lean on someone when he walks and how he rolls off the couch and crawls to a chair to pull himself up to lean on furniture to walk around the house. Also, he sits in front of the refrigerator on the floor to get things out of it or to brush his teeth in the bathroom on the floor.

One night, he said he wanted to go home. He feels he is a burden, but he is a blessing. I see God at work through him daily. He says he can't talk or write so what good does his intelligence do, and I tell him how he encourages and inspires others.

So yesterday morning, one of my insureds went to the house and talked with him and told him how good he thought he was doing. Then later, another spent four hours talking to him and reading scripture and both my sisters popped in to see him, too. And then he got a message from an older lady at church with a beautiful prayer for him.

April 7, 2013

Dear Russell,

The first of the month Brian was disappointed with the infectious disease doctor he went to. The man made fun of the Lyme disease doctor and told Brian to get back to the Cleveland Clinic—that there was no way he could have gotten better. Of course, Brian was not pleased with a doctor who would put down another doctor. But he did get depressed.

Thursday, Brian was very down and wanted to go home to heaven.

Friday morning, he woke up a big smile. He was very calm. His sinus stopped draining, and he has his hope again. Then Friday evening, he told me he wanted to drive to the dance. I really prayed then. LOL. He drove some back roads and then let me drive. At the dance, he did a slow rumba about four times. One the way home, he was so happy. He kept repeating, "I drove. I danced. I spoke."

To Russell

We saw Dr. Charles Resseger for allergies to help the sinus drainage, because the more he drains, the more he slurs. Dr Resseger tested him for Epstein-Barr virus and on the test one to five, it came out over that for activity. We see him Friday to see if he is treating that with peptide shots.

He thinks Brian should continue to see Dr. J also, since he is top in the country for Lyme disease.

The speech department says one side of his tongue is weaker than the other.

I feel his legs and hands have worsened. He has troubles scooting up in bed. He still does his physical and speech exercises.

Brian has stopped his herbal treatments and is just on the once-a-day vitamins; B complex, Biaxin, Rocephin, and probiotics. He has gained some muscle in his calf.

He is more tired than he has been. Physical Therapy is going well.

I found solace in writing poems, as I had done so much of my life.

April 9, 2013

It's not supposed to be
My son, instead of me.
I should be the one.
How can this be?
From healthy,
To diseased.
From a wholesome
Strong young man.
Hope lifts me high.
I soar alone.
When things are down.
I trust His love.
He sees the end.
I see the now.
I try to hope
But don't know how.
The road is rough.
The times are hard.
Where would I be,
Without my Lord?

April 27, 2013

Lord,
He wants to die.
Who am I to hold him back?
He wants to go home.
He wants to be with You.
Sure, it saddens me to hear these words.
It saddens me to lose Brian.

But the joy he will have
When he sees you
Face to face.
And
Away and isolated from the world.
From the ones he loves,
Learning new ways,
New values
Away,
But not alone.

May 4, 2013

Dear heavenly Father,

It's a new day, Lord. Brian fell down yesterday on the front steps. Lord, thank You that he
didn't fall into the block of concrete Bill and Joe
had torn out.

Lord, I pray for joy to return to Brian. Joy
and hope. He needs that.

You are my heavenly, Abba, and Daddy, and
I don't want to see anyone hurt, especially my
Brian.

Abba Daddy, I think you are the greatest,
I know.

I am overwhelmed, but where would I be
without God and the friends He has placed in
our lives. You, my friend, is one of those dear
friends. Thank you.

June 1, 2013

Hi Russell,

Brian went down on his knees today. He thinks he'll need a wheelchair soon. Frowning face.

My friend, Barb, from high school suggested to Brian that he go on disability and get his hover round and such while he can, but Brian is too proud. I hope the shot that he gets Friday helps some. It is so sad to talk to him and not understand him. To see his weak legs.

Brian has gone to a graduation tonight and then on to a game with the guys. At least he is still able to get out.

June 2, 2013

He wants a wheelchair. He's tired. He's weak. He's falling down. I am sad, Lord. Sad for Brian—sad for me.

Confused about the future. Kind of scared—unsure of my footing.

Wanting to look chipper; to shine, to be strong.

Sometimes, tired and reaching for time. Time flies.

There are not enough hours in a day for what needs done.

To Russell,

Brian isn't doing well this week. He's down to 105 pounds. With tears in his eyes at night when we are alone, he tells me he wants to go home.

He says he doesn't want to live like this. I am still hoping the peptide shots will help. He gets another one Friday at 10:00 a.m.

June 24, 2013

Lord,

My Jehovah, Jireh. Your grace is sufficient for me. You are the good shepherd of Brain. You are the King of kings.

King Jesus, send your angel to watch over Russell and Brian L. Especially be with Brian, my son, in his journey of death or if you chose, life.

June 25, 2013

Dear God,

Good morning, Jesus. A new day dawning. Cuddles came home again today. Brian will be glad.

Father, Brian wants me to put his car in my name. He says he will never drive again. Thank You that he is willing to give it over. But it is hard to see him this way.

Lord, You know what is happening with Brian. Be with my Brian with the process. It has to be tough knowing you are leaving the families to the unknown. It is a transition that all make, but wow. What a journey.

July 27, 2013

Lord, I am hurting badly, seeing Brian hurting. He even talked about how he should go to a nursing home. No way, Lord! He isn't that bad. I don't want him away from me. No, no, no! Not a nursing home. Lord, I hurt for him. I haven't been able to think or do.

Thank You for the help. Lord, lift me up. Lift Brian up, and let us stand on heaven;'s high and holy land. Help!

July 31, 2013 Facebook posts

Alice Stuckey

Brian has been sobbing a lot this evening and crying that God doesn't love him. He thinks he will be dead by his birthday, September 12th. Brian says he can't remember being well. He wakes up about 4:00 a.m. every morning, crying.

August 1, 2013, Norwalk, Ohio

Stayed in the house all day and did insurance work from there. I don't want to leave Brian alone anymore. I have bells set up in his bed room and bathroom and living room to ring to call me.

August 3, 2013

Lord,

This has been the roughest week so far. Brian giving up. Brian lying in bed, saying he will not go anywhere. Him crying and sobbing uncontrollably. He said he lost his independence when hospice came. Lord, what am I to do? I left home alone last night, because he wanted me to go, and I am alone today, because he wants to be independent. (sad face)

My chapel friends, insureds, friends, hospice, and doctors have been very supportive. Thank You, Lord. I need Your helpers. I am weak, but You are strong. I pray You will be glorified in all of this. Thank You, Jesus, please keep Brian's spirits up.

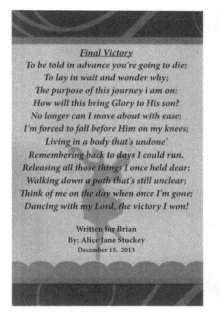

In Life, In Death, Brian Gives Honor To God

August 5, 2013

Brian has been depressed, which I would say is normal, facing death. He hates change and hates his hospital bed and furniture moved or removed for his safety. He also hates having so much company, but I guess I can't blame him for that, since he has so many, many friends who love him. He has high school friends, church friends, insureds, youth—from the youth groups he has been a leader in, gaming friends, and even a friend who has been his friend since infancy. His friend, Mike, was born eight days before him, and he calls Brian his other brother from a different mother and father.

Brian says "no more good days" since hospice came in. They really are not here all that much, and really only visit with him right now. He still wants Mom to bathe him and dress him and give him his meds and tuck him in and get up at night with him and fix his meals. I am thankful to the Lord, that He has given me good health to be able to care for Brian. Brian doesn't want to go to church or out to eat anymore and wants to give up painting his miniatures or doing little things he used to do. I am told that is the anger stage of grief. (I don't like this grief experience.)

Our ramp is not built yet, so his friend, Joe, has come over to help me get him to the car for church. He just picks him up and carries him. Two of our four pastors have been over to visit Brian. The team leaders of the high school youth group came out to move his bed out to put the hospital bed in. That team of leaders, and some others are planning a surprise walk through his life party for him sometime in September.

Dr. Robinson says he needs 24/7 care now because he is such high risk of falling and breaking his bone. He has lost all his muscle, and he looks like his skin is stretched right over the bones of the skeleton. Two of my friends who are in the medical field, one a doctor and one a PT, told me they think Brian may have six to eight months at most, and since his little flap that keeps from going into the lungs is weak, he could get pneumonia and die much sooner. It is a sad time for all of us, but I am trusting God. I don't understand but He is keeping me strong.

Facebook post.

August 15, 2013, Norwalk, Ohio

I do not know if I am going to be going to church except on greeting days for a while. Brian's butt hurts him to sit too long. I have to have someone with Brian at all times. I understand hospice cannot be here more often until it is closer to the end or something like that, and Brian will not let the nurse aides do anything but visit, and he doesn't like the visits, so I guess they will be stopping that for now until later.

Even if I run out to the office, I tell him I will be right back in the house in a few minutes. When I have to work, I have to call on friends to sit with him. And then I can't be gone long, because I am the only one he allows to hold the urinal for him. Also, I am one usually of the only ones who moves him around. Sometimes, Cindy or Bill helps me. Of course, Chris helps, and Joe can do it all himself. But Joe is at the Huron County Fair this week and then he starts college. It is getting very hard for me to move him. I am afraid I will be needing more help very soon. It took most my day up caring for him yesterday. Didn't get to my insurance work until after we closed the office.

When friends come to see him, he tires out so easily. I think it is because he feels he has to put on a smile and a good front. Anyone wanting to come and sit while I have to work or sit with me to help move Brian or who has any suggestions on what would make it easier for me to give him the care he needs would be appreciated.

I do covet your prayers. I thank God daily for the friends who love and care about Brian. May His name be glorified!

August 19, 2013, Norwalk, Ohio

No sleep for Mom tonight. Brian could not get comfortable and kept ringing his bell. Twice, I found him trying to sit up with his feet off the bed. (I had given him Ambien, so I do not know if he even knew what he was doing.) Then he said his allergies were bothering him, and the phlegm was choking him, and he wanted to go back out to the couch to sleep. I got him out there, but he still couldn't get comfortable, so I rolled him on the floor with me to sleep. He is sleeping now but my mind is racing, and I am not sleeping. Abba, Father, Daddy, you're the best dad on the block. You never go to sleep at night. You're with me round the clock.

August 22, 2013, Norwalk, Ohio

Brian's back has been hurting the past few days, and he can't get comfortable sitting or lying in his bed. I wish I knew how to lay him, so he would feel comfortable. Things we take for granted like rolling over in bed, sitting up, walking, talking are all too hard for him. So sad to see him like this, but, God is going to give him a new body, and he will be dancing and singing in heaven.

The end of August, Brian couldn't get his breath, so once more, hospice sent him to the unit. Of course, Mom went with him. I didn't want him to feel abandoned or if it was his time, to die alone.

August 28, 2013

Brian is sleeping lightly now. He just woke up and told me to shut the door. He seems to think he will not go home from here. I keep telling him that is not so.

True Hero
The body may change
But the man does not.
True worth of the man
Is what is inside and,
Not what's without

It's easy to be a hero
When life is going well,
But when life strikes a blow,
It's the ture hero
That you know.

The true hero is persistent,
In the way he faces loss.
He stands to face the enemy,
And leans upon The Cross!

The true hero is seen
Inside a man's heart.
You see the true hero in the end,
And not the start!

Written for Brian
By: Alice Jane Stuckey
June 23, 2013

In Loving Memory Of
Brian Keith Stuckey

Date Of Birth
September 12, 1971
Sandusky, Ohio

Entered Into Rest
December 29, 2013
Norwalk, Ohio

Funeral Service
January 3, 2014
1:00 pm
The Chapel North Campus

Officiating
Rev. Eric Lapata
Rev. Todd Nielsen

Final Resting Place
Milan Cemetery
Milan, Ohio

Arrangements By
Groff Funeral Homes & Crematory
Sandusky, Ohio

Brian Wanted to Die A Hero, But He Never
Saw Himself As the One He Was!

August 28, 2013

Brian has been up and down all night. He has me getting up with him every forty-five minutes to an hour, just like at home. They have given him pain meds and sleeping meds, but he is still having problems getting comfortable.

August 29, 2013

We are still at Firelands S. Campus Hospice center. Brian is sleeping now. I had a good four hours of sleep tonight and will probably sleep more in a little bit.

We've had lots of friends and family visit here. So much support. I couldn't list everyone, but you know who you are.

We had some excitement last evening. I went to go home to get insurance work done, clean clothes, and eat at my sister's. By the time I got there, I had a phone call from Ashley saying Brian wanted to go home now. He wanted me to go back to the hospital right away, so I did. When I got back, he decided he would stay at least tonight.

Cindy stayed with Brian while I drove home where I had Gary waiting to take Russell's call. (No call came tonight.) Gary saw I was tired, so he drove me back over here. We will see what tomorrow brings. Brian believes he is going to die here and will not get a chance to go back to the house again.

This one thing I know, God who started a good work in Brian will see it to completion. He is and was and is to come. My God is alive. If Jesus is for us, then, who can stand against us?

September 1, 2013

We are finding that God has even purposed Brian and myself to be in this hospice unit at this time and this point of his disease. There have been special visitors God has sent to minister to us, but also visitors for us to love on and minister to.

We met a lady from Milan who recognized us, but we don't know. Her mother died of ALS, and she was able to tell Brian how they have something, so he will not suffer when he passes.

And I have met the families of the patients up here. One special person I met last night is Marsha. She is here from New Mexico. Her dad is dying and needs prayer for peace that only God can give. He wants to die now! The Holy Spirit has His seal upon him, and Satan cannot have him. I told Marsha Satan knows this, but he is trying to rob her dad of his peace and joy. Marsha and I talked, and she wants to go to church with me in the morning if she has someone to sit with her dad. Thank you, God, for opportunities to be about Your work. Thank You for giving us something to dwell on besides our own suffering. Bless these people who have stepped into our path this week.

While I was in Brian's room, I wrote emails to his friends to let them know that the youth leaders were planning a surprise hero forty-second birthday party for him. Brian always wanted to die a hero and now he said, he never would get to do that. How wrong he was!

Finally, on Labor Day we got to go home.

September 7, 2013, Norwalk, Ohio

Brian woke me up last night to ask me about a grave plot. Tough things to talk to your son about, but that is something I want to be there to help him through. I am so blessed to have a son who shares everything—every thought with me. Thank You, Jesus

September 10, 2013, Norwalk, Ohio

Just up thinking some things over that have happened recently. Nothing makes sense to me except that I am not doing a good job of things here. Kind of sad tonight. Kind of confused. (And that is okay—I am human, and I am loved by an awesome Father.) Our futures are unknown, and surprises happen daily. Praise God that I don't have to know the whys and wherefores. God handles that. Thank God, that He is bigger than all my thoughts.

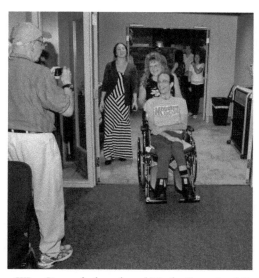

Brian Was Overwhelmed and Truly Surprised By the
Junior and Senior High Education Department at
Church Honoring Him on His 42nd Birthday

September 27, 2013, Norwalk, Ohio

Brian and our dog, T-Bone, were up most the
night. Brian didn't want to take the morphine
because it makes his brain foggy, and T-bone has
a bad, painful ear. I'd get one resting, and the
other one would start in. God please give both of
them rest today.

Brian loves his new chair. Joe Taylor came by
yesterday in the morning, and Jason Steckel came
by in the evening and talked to Brian and shared
scripture with him about dying and the heavenly
Father who loves him. What a blessing to have
men and women of God in our lives.

My nieces did their college homework here
while Brian watched movies with them. I am

thankful for the time people sit with him. I am so far behind on my accounting for the office and other paperwork. No complaints, just fact. Brian is the most important thing right now. I want to cherish every minute and make memories.

Thanks to Ashley for coming by and working with Brian while I was in the office in the afternoon. Thanks for working with Brian's stretches and your encouragement.

Chris Pleasnick, our wonderful friend and PT, came by after she got off work and did stretches and showed me how to use the lift and visited with both Brian and me. Then Billie Jo brought supper, and the nurse dropped off medication, and Cindy came for the evening.

I know God is using this time for all of us to grow closer to Him and to share His love. Thank You, Jesus, for allowing us to be a part of Your story.

September 28, 2013, Norwalk, Ohio

Brian didn't want to go to sleep last night. He said he had never been in so much pain. He was sure he would die. He sat on the couch and typed on his iPad, "Please accept Jesus, Dad."

When Bill went to bed, he asked me to have his dad stay up with him. I got Bill out of bed. Then after a bit, we put Brian in bed and Brian and I talked. Then, he asked me for his Ambien. His night was restless, and I slept on the floor beside the bed.

Lord, only You know when the time will be for Brian to go home to You. I pray for comfort for Brian. I pray for rest for him. Lord, please give him the peace that passes understanding. Please help Bill to understand and accept Brian's request. I know all things are possible with You. It is even possible that Bill would someday accept You.

What a mighty God we serve! I may not understand Your ways, but I know they are always right and just.

October 8, 2013, Norwalk, Ohio

All is well that ends well. I was up with Brian till five this morning. I finished the night on the floor beside his bed. He was so sick last night. Then once the medicine started to work, he started vomiting also. It is very hard when he throws up, because he cannot hold himself up to lean over. Someone has to be there to hold him in a sitting position and to hold the pan for him. I think he will feel better now when he wakes up. He is a real trooper though, taking medicine that tastes terrible. I don't know if I could do that. Yuck.

I am so thankful that Joseph Claus came after college last night and was here to help me most the night. Joe has been a real help and comfort these past few years.

Billie Jo Houghtlen brought us roast for supper last night. And Martha Taylor has said she will sit with Brian, Wednesday, so the blessings just keep on flowing from our Father's throne. Thank You, Jesus.

October 10, 2013, Norwalk, Ohio

Brian has had an upset stomach and throwing up at night since the hospice nurse was here earlier in the week. Last night, he threw up five times from 11:00–3:00. I called hospice again and the nurse was out here from 4:00–6:30. He is sleeping now. I am up and dressed for work and whatever the day holds. The nurse says I need a break and help, but you know you do what you have to do. She asked me how I did all I do, and I told her it is by the power of God. He is my strength. What a mighty God I serve!

October 11, 2013

Brian is sleeping well. I am glad he agreed to come up to the unit. We are in a smaller room than last time, and my chair is not as comfortable as the couch was last time, but it is good we are here. Father, my great physician, please get Brian comfortable so he can go home and enjoy the new porch his dad made for him. Please send helpers to aid me in lifting him and sitting with him, that he feels comfortable with. I do my best, but this old lady is not as strong as she once was. She is not as independent as she has always thought she was. I guess Brian and I are learning that lesson together. We cannot always be the one to rescue. Sometimes, we need rescued too.

Leaning, leaning, leaning on the everlasting arms.

October 12, 2013

I had a good night. Both Brian and I slept all through the night. It looks like he is getting back to functional. If he keeps this up, he will get to go home soon. Not today, but maybe some time tomorrow or Monday. The staff with us here has been great. Thank you, God, for this medical team.

One of the chaplains came by Brian's room last evening and talked with Brian and saw his book from the party and the YouTube video which I told him to look up as "Man with ALS and Brian Stuckey" to share with others. He told me later that he had to step out because he got teary-eyed. He told me he could just see Jesus's love and spirit shining through Brian. He said even when he got all that praise, he turned the glory to God and not himself. Oh, his mama is so proud of his spirit for Christ!

October 12, 2013

Dr. Preston was just in, and he is releasing Brian today. When all the paperwork is done and the ambulance comes, we will go home. It won't be until the afternoon or evening, but he is smiling

October 14, 2013, Norwalk, Ohio

Brian didn't sleep well last night. He was restless and could not get comfortable. I slept on the floor beside his bed. I have to work the office today, so Gary B. is coming to sit this morning, and my sister, Lucy, will sit this afternoon. (They will have to call me to move Brian.) Thank You, Jesus, for those who come to sit.

October 17, 2013, Norwalk, Ohio

Great news! Hospice has lifted its restriction on Brian's care. Home health care will be out starting tomorrow. Then, two former health aides have offered to volunteer to help me with him on their days off, and one man, whose brother in law died of ALS, is willing to help some days. Ted is very spiritual and very capable of caring for Brian. I have some leads to other people who are qualified to care for Brian, so things are looking up! ☺ Thank You, Jesus! Also, Gary contacted United Way to get some help, and they are looking in to some things. Thank you, everyone, for your prayers. I need all the help I can get. A big *Thank You* to Martha Tayler who sat with Brian today and to my sister, Lucy who got him another plastic mug to drink out of and went after some of my meds.

Lord, I am feeling uplifted and encouraged today with the prospect of help coming my way. Thank You, Jesus.

October 25, 2013, Norwalk, Ohio

Brian has been really sleeping a lot this week. Today, he seemed almost comatose. I called hospice and also ALS association was out here to try to help Brian with some communication devices, but he was really too out of it to care. I was really worried about him. I am sitting in his room beside him while he sleeps. I can only imagine what he is thinking or doing in his mind.

Ted Thompson sat with Brian today for the first time. Ted is Tom Stalling's brother-in-law.

November 5, 2013, Norwalk, Ohio

Brian has been in some pain lately and crying some. I wish I could take his sadness and pain on myself. I hate to see him go through this. I know God hates to see his pain too. He loves Brian more than I could even begin to. Heavenly Father, please be merciful to Brian tonight and grant him a peaceful night of rest. Please, Lord. I hate to see him linger in pain, both physically and emotionally. How much more must he take before he can dance again with You in heaven?

My sister, Lucy, came up and sat with Brian after Ted left today.

Prayers are appreciated right now. I don't know how to comfort Brian. I know our Father in heaven holds him in the palm of His hand. Praise be to God our Father. He is the One True God!

November 10, 2013, Norwalk, Ohio

What an amazing day! Ashley Wilson sat with Brian while I worked in the office, and the others from two small groups from the church cut and split wood with Bill from 9:00–12:00 yesterday. How blessed we are! That will give him a good start on his winter wood now. Joe Claus was benefitted by the love shown also. He is the one who has been helping Bill with all the projects that Brian and Bill used to do. Thank you, everyone, for your help. Glory and praise be to God for His faithful servants!

November 11, 2013, Norwalk, Ohio

We had to put Brian's dog, T-bone, to sleep today. Of course, with Brian's emotions very unstable, he cried every time he thought of T-bone.

November 19, 2013, Norwalk, Ohio

This morning, Brian asked for his iPad and typed, "I'm sorry I was up so much. I don't deserve you."

I told him God placed me here for him, and as I was caring for him, I was worshipping God. I also told him I love him and wanted to be here for him and reminded him that he would do the same for me, if I were ill.

God, help me to remember everything I do throughout this day is worship to You. Open my eyes to those needs around me you want me to meet. Fill me with Your Spirit.

November 22, 2013, Norwalk, Ohio

Feeling sad for Brian this morning. Yesterday, he was crying and typed how disappointed he was that some of his good friends had not been to see him. I know he cannot talk, but he can listen and smile and laugh and if any of you have the time in the next month or so, I would appreciate it if you would visit or drop him a note in the mail or post something here for me to print off for him to read. I do realize this is a very busy time of year with the holidays. Brian needs the body of Christ to surround him with the Father's love. Thank you so much for those of you who can do this. Thank you to all of you who continually pray for Brian and me and especially for Bill.

November 25, 2013, Norwalk, Ohio

I had to tell Brian this morning that his good friend and fellow dancer Mr. Bill Walker passed away, yesterday morning. He had fallen down the steps at a dance. I understand he never woke up. Of course, Brian cried off and on all day. Please pray for him to calm down.

December 3, 2013

Brian has been up the last two nights so much that this evening when I sat down beside him on the floor, I zonked out. He had a lot of saliva to suction out those nights. Hope he is better tonight. Ken and Jen Rawlson came by to see Brian today for a bit. He was glad to see them. He loves to see his friends.

God is good. Even though I am only human and need my sleep, God never sleeps. He is so available. Wonderful Counselor, Holy Spirit, living inside of each of His children.

December 3, 2013, Norwalk, Ohio

A few things this morning. Yesterday, Brian was telling me all he can do anymore is to watch videos. The next thing is he hates feeling so helpless. Then last evening, I fell asleep on the floor beside the couch, and he was very frustrated with me. I don't mean to fall asleep on him, but after the last three nights up (counting last night), when I sit down, I can hardly keep my eyes open or wake up. Of course, Bill and Joe were here so he was not alone. But he wanted Maaa. This birthing into heaven is a lot harder and more painful than his first birth into this world. Pray for comfort for Brian both spiritual and physical. Pray for strength that only comes from on high for me. Our God is good and just, and He will hear and come to our aide.

December 13, 2013, Norwalk, Ohio

Brian has been pretty sick the past few days. I didn't get to sleep till 6:30 yesterday morning and had to open the agency at 9:00. Today is day 7 and we are still waiting on a BM. Poor kid, he is miserable and scared he won't be able to.

At least he slept some last evening. The night before he went from the couch to the bed to the floor to the bed to the floor to the couch and wanted drinks etc., he is dead weight, so it is tough sitting him up for a drink and helping him hold the cup. And moving him off the floor is almost impossible for one person. But I guess I wasn't one person because the Holy Spirit lives inside of me. Looks like the two of us make a good team.

Thank You, dear Jesus for this precious journey I am on. Thank You for what you are doing through all of this. I can't wait to see the results when I get to heaven.

"We will understand it better by and by. By and by, when the morning comes. By and by when the Saints are gathered home... We will understand it better by and by."

December 16, 2013, Norwalk, Ohio

Bill Fox, the hospice volunteer, called me in the house because Brian was crying today. He said his back hurt but then he typed that he thought he was going to die this week. Amber, our nurse, came out and checked him. She said he is modeling and that his blood pressure is low. She said they usually know when they are going to die. She also said this could be the new normal for Brian. He asked for more morphine, and he is sleeping now. I didn't think I would panic but I did when he told me that. I asked Bill what the nurse told him, but he didn't seem to get the message I did from her. He just thought Brian is getting a little worse.

Father of peace and understanding, grant us the peace that only You can give. Comfort Brian with Your Holy Spirit. Comfort those of us who are left behind grieving. But not grieving as those who have no hope but grieving for our loss. Rejoicing for his gain. It is so hard to imagine life without Brian in his earthly body. It all seems so unreal.

With the Poem, "Final Victory" on the Back of his Grave Marker, Brian Leaves His Witness of Faith to All Who Pass By

December 17, 2013, Norwalk, Ohio

Chris Pleasasnik, Joseph Claus, and Cindy Haycook came to see Brian tonight. Chris comforted Brian as only Chris can. She is so in tuned with him. After massaging his feet and working his arms and everything and talking to him, he seems a lot better! He told her he was scared cause he like zoned out. He now thinks he will be okay for a while, and he may not go up to hospice. He will see how it is going when they call with a bed. He said he was really scared he was going to die. My dear friend, Chris, how can I ever thank God enough for putting her in our lives for this time?

Thanks to all of you who have sent your love and prayers today. A special thanks to Eric and Paula for calling to check up on Brian. The journey gets harder and harder when I don't know what to do, but your prayers and comfort are such a sign of God's presence.

December 17, 2013, Norwalk, Ohio

How often has he cried out to you?
"Take me home."
How often has he said he just
wants to die.
Have I missed his words?
Has he cried alone
For you to take him home?
I want to be there for him;
I want to lift his spirits
I want to point to Jesus.
Love him with words unspoken
Listen for what is broken?
I want to calm his fears
Dry his tears
I want to hold him close
And whisper words of comfort
Tell him it's all right
And hold him tight
Do you hear his cries?
Do you hear his pleas?
Won't you move, God?
Won't you move, God?
I beg you,
Move, God.

Written for Brian Stuckey by his mom
Alice Jane Stuckey
April 9, 2013

December 21, 2013, Norwalk, Ohio

How blessed we are with God's amazing abun-
dant surpassing all we could have asked or hoped

for provision. He has used so many of you to be His hands and feet in service to us, part of the body of Christ. Just today, Eric called from Michigan to say that Dr. Paushauer heard Brian's eye was bothering him, and the doctor and Bev came out to look at it and take care of it. Chris P. was sitting here with Brian while I worked the agency, and she got instructions on what I need to do. Earlier in the day, Carrie M. Ott and her children came and sang and talked with Brian while I was in the office. Larry Waaland went shopping for Bill's Christmas presents. Cheryle Olson is picking up some videos I have at the Exchange. All my posts on Facebook represent just a few of the people God is using for us on our journey. If I had one request of all of you, is to go out and do this for others for the sake of Jesus. There are so many who do not have the love or support that we have had. My heart aches for them.

December 23, 2013, Norwalk, Ohio

Back with the living. Had flu and never got off the floor for over twenty-four hours except to throw up. Sure do feel better except for the aches and pains from laying on the floor so long. Bill and Joe Claus were real troopers and helped me with Brian. I think the funniest thing that happened was when Bill went to town, Brian rolled off the couch and trapped me under him. We had to wait about twenty minutes for Bill to come home and lift Brian off of me. At least Brian had a soft cushion to land on.

Barbara Price Maher to Alice Stuckey
December 24, 2013

A letter to Brian, you are so on my mind! I want to tell you of my memories when you were born and just how proud you made your mother. She glowed with happiness showing the motherly love that is so unique. With songs, poems, and rhyme, she started you into the world. Your first dance was with your mom holding her lovely boy in her arms, singing songs of praise and thankfulness for you. And you smiled! I remember you walking up to my door with your tote in hand, full of toys you loved, books, and of course, a snack and drink. You and you mom perfect examples of love. Your mother would instruct, sing and hop with you. You played with my kids. And of course, you would smile, shy, of course. Your mom would dance, and your eyes would light up with love that she taught you. She would smile proud of your steps to manhood. Last summer, I saw you again. Your smile is contagious. You showed me your dance and you, the young man, taught me lessons. I use these lessons every day. To smile, through it all. You and your mom teach well young man. Your mom has taught me so much as a young mother and a mature woman. You taught me to be brave and above all, to dance through the struggle to make it easier. I thank you.

December 24, 2013, Norwalk, Ohio

Brian has continuous care at home with hospice after having an episode early this morning.

Ashley Keeton is with Karina Haycook and three others.
December 25, 2013

So blessed to see another miracle from Brian Stuckey this afternoon. 🤍♡ Being so weak, he still lifted both his arms up in the air, even lifting almost over his head. He still gives us thumbs up, and he will never lose his smile, that one of a kind smile. When my mom was rubbing his legs, she also felt him lift his leg on his own a little bit, trying to. Thankful to be able to see Brian for Christmas this year. 🤍♡🌲🎄

As the High School Worship Leader, Zac Yonek, and His Friend, Eric Lapata, Sing, "Our God Is Greater," Joined Them By Raising His Arm in Praise- A True Miracle!

December 25, 2013, Norwalk, Ohio

Bittersweet Christmas today. Brian is declining but friends and family have been so wonderful to us today. Please pray for comfort and peace for Brian. I will try to post more tonight.

December 26, 2013, Norwalk, Ohio

I've been up since 8:00 yesterday morning. Brian is not doing well. I see his knuckles turning gray. His jaws are clenched, and so I can only use a syringe to try to get meds down or liquids. He has different problems breathing and communicating. I really don't know how to describe this. He still will try to squeeze my hand, and he will do a little thumbs-up sometimes, but it is so weak. He sleeps with his eyes open or stares into space. I have tried to post pics of yesterday, and God has been so good to send so much family and support of friends through here the past two days. Bill does not seem to understand how bad Brian is right now, and Brian, when he can get his questions out on iPad with me guessing, has asked if he is worse and what are hospice goals and things. Thank You, God for the wonderful things and the way lives have been touched even during these two days. One nurse told me she could not believe how changed her life will be because of the three short hours she spent with us the first day she came in the middle of the night. She says her life will never be the same after meeting our family. Praise God.

December 26, 2013, Norwalk, Ohio

Dr. Robinson just left, and he said it will be a few hours to a few days. Making calls and sharing this with others on Facebook.

December 27, 2013

Miracles still tonight with Brian. When some prayers were said, he nodded his head that he could see the angels. Out of nowhere, twice, he raised his arm up straight in the air, for his dad. My boyfriend Mike surprised us and came by, and with him he brought Mountain Dew for everyone to drink with Brian. We put some Mountain Dew in cap for nurse to dip and sponge like stick and swabbed it around Brian's lips/mouth... he pursed his lips around it tightly!!!!! These are miracles, because Brian has been unresponsive, yet was able to still make us proud.

December 28, 2013

Brian still is fighting hard tonight and throughout today. He was making more noises today and reaching his arms up. He motioned his one arm up towards his mouth multiple times, so we swabbed some Mountain Dew in his mouth, he did purse his lips around it. He had worship songs being sung for him and everyone together by Zach Yonek and his sister. He did respond to some songs. Earlier when I played some songs on computer, it looked as though he had some tears in his eye, as if he was praising the only way he could and was so happy. Later tonight, he has become unresponsive and making no movements to anything. His heart is still beating quickly and working hard. Praying that Brian can finally be free again.

December 28, 2013

Brian is still inspiring others even as his earthly body continues to weaken. Still unresponsive tonight. His heart continues to work hard. His tongue has started to thrust a little bit tonight. His breathing is shallow, but he keeps holding on. God still has a purpose for our hero. Thank you for all your prayers. Please continue, for his peace and comfort as he dances his way to heaven.

Ken Rawson

December 29, 2013

Bittersweet feelings today as I heard about my friend Brian Stuckey passing away at 5:05 AM this morning. Brian was an amazing, humble, and generous friend and youth worker. I will truly never forget him.

What blows me away even more are the number of people who were woken up in the middle of the night and felt compelled to pray for Brian and Alice Stuckey last night. So powerful. So comforting. So mind-blowing!

What an inspiring year for us all. As this new year approaches, we have so much to remember and cherish. Brian has been through so much in this past year and has touched so many lives. Through his journey, his battle, his life, he has made such an impact on others. His miracles, his struggles, his faith, and his strength through it all. May the coming of 2014 give all of us inspiration to love more, extend grace more, have more faith, cherish more, treasure more, bless more, pray more, and remember more. *Because* of Brian, we are able to see each day as a blessing, a day to do what you love, be with those you love, and be kind. Think of others before thinking of yourself. Appreciate each moment you are given. Keep your passions no matter the matter the struggle and keep your faith strong when you begin to lose hope. In sadness, there is happiness. In darkness, there is light. Thank you, Brian for being my best friend, my hero.

obituaries

BRIAN KEITH STUCKEY
SEPT. 12, 1971-DEC. 29, 2013

SANDUSKY

Brian Keith Stuckey, 42, has continued his Christmas celebration with his big brother Jesus. He arrived at his Heavenly Father's house at 5:05 a.m. Sunday, Dec. 29, 2013, where he will enjoy eternity with his friends and family who have gone on before him.

Stuckey

Brian had been on loan to his mother, Alice (Risdon) Stuckey, and father, William A. Stuckey, since Sept. 12, 1971.

He attended St. Mary's Elementary and St. Paul's High School of Norwalk, where he graduated in 1989. He went to Ohio Valley College in Parkersburg, W.Va. Brian spent his time here on earth going about his Heavenly Father's business, serving as a youth leader for the church from the age of 18 until his final breath. He also served God through his work in retail at Ames and Waldenbooks, and as an insurance agent at the Stuckey Agency. Brian's numerous talents and interests allowed him to enjoy farm and building projects with his dad, exploring history, gaming, dancing, writing and much more.

In addition to his parents, Brian is survived by aunts, Nancy Jean Stuckey, Nancy Lee Stuckey, Jean (Risdon) Bauer and her husband Dick and Lucille (Risdon) Blake; special cousin, Noel Bauer Steel and her loving children; nine other cousins and members of the Stuckey and Bauer families. Although he was thought to be an only child by the world, Brian leaves behind too many spiritual brothers, sisters and friends to count.

Brian is being welcomed into Heaven by paternal grandparents, Louis Stuckey Sr. in 1985, Vera (Chaffee) Stuckey in 1965; maternal grandparents, Glenn F. Risdon in 2008, Edna (Delfing) Risdon in 2003, and Pearl Marie (Klucas) Risdon in 1953; his uncles Louis "Sonny" Stuckey in 2004 and Jim Blake in 2003; cousin and friend, Sherry Bauer in 1990; and his good friend, photographer and dancer Mr. Bil Walker, earlier this month.

Friends may call 2-4 p.m. and 6-8 p.m. Thursday, Jan. 2, at the Chapel North Campus, 4444 Galloway Rd., Sandusky. Friends may also call from noon Friday, Jan. 3, until funeral services at 1 p.m. at the Chapel with the Rev. Eric Lapata and the Rev. Todd Nielsen presiding.

Condolences may be shared at grofffuneralhomes.com.

Contributions in Brian's memory may be made to The ALS Association, 6155 Rockside Rd., Independence, OH 44131, The Chapel, 4444 Galloway Rd., Sandusky, OH 44870, Black Tie Dance Studio, 120 E. Adams St., Sandusky, OH 44870, or to the Cleveland Foodbank, 15500 S. Waterloo Rd., Cleveland, OH 44110.

Out of respect for Brian, the Stuckey Agency will be closed Friday, Jan. 3, to allow his friends and co-workers to process their grief.

Christmas Celebration, Here and There

December 29, 2013, 5:05 a.m.

2 Timothy 4:7-8 I have fought the good fight, I have finished the race, I have kept the faith. Now there is in store for me the crown of righteousness, which the Lord, the righteous Judge, will award to me on that day—and not only to me, but also to all who have longed for his appearing.

Brian's Final Challenge

Though we cannot see it with our eyes, we feel the air in our lungs and wind in our face and we believe it exists.

So it has been with Jesus the past three years of Brian's journey home. I've seen my Jesus through the willing hands and hearts of family and friends coming along side of Bill and myself, allowing Jesus to wrap himself up in your hands and legs and words to minister to Bill and myself.

Through those who stepped up to take on responsibilities that Bill once depended on Brian to do, I have seen my Jesus. I've seen him in the touch of your hands, the wheels of your cars, the person behind the weed wacker, the visits, the cards, a surprise birthday party, food delivered, people sitting with Brian so I could take care of my other responsibilities Through 15 men and women cutting firewood with Bill and 4 ladies sorting potatoes with Bill. I've seen him in the hands of doctors who treated him and in a physical theripist who has given her heart and friendship not only to Brian but to myself and my husband. I've seen my Lord in Joe who sat through the nights with Brian and worked along sit of Bill on his projects through the day.

As Nick Betchtal, one of Brian's youths told Brian just before taking his last breath, "Having experience all of this, how could I not believe. I want to see you in heaven."

And i know Brian wants to see each of you, his friends and family there, as well. Thank you for showing me Jesus in the Flesh.

After knowing the man my son Brian was and his love for Jesus, How can you not believe?

The Final Challenge

About the Author

Alice Jane Stuckey grew up in the fifties on a dairy farm.

She began writing poems and short stories after being given a writing assignment by her eighth-grade teacher.

It has been a lifelong practice of hers to write out her prayers in the morning over coffee.

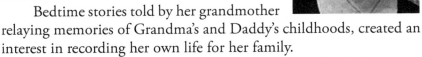

Bedtime stories told by her grandmother relaying memories of Grandma's and Daddy's childhoods, created an interest in recording her own life for her family.

Alice grew up going to church and Sunday school. She never doubted the existence of Christ.

Alice accepted Christ as her Lord and Savior and began her own personal relationship with Him at a youth rally when she was sixteen.

Leaning on the strength only Jesus could provide through life's struggles, Alice learned she could have a deep, trusting relationship with Him. He is her strength and hope.

Brian said when Christ healed him, he wanted to give his testimony to others so they could see what a mighty God he served. On December 29, 2013, the Lord, restored him to complete wholeness. As his mother, I am honored to share his amazing faith. I pray you will be encouraged, as I have been to draw close to God. He will never leave you or forsake you. He catches your tears in a vial. Your name is engraved in the palm of his hand.

CPSIA information can be obtained
at www.ICGtesting.com
Printed in the USA
BVHW091913140619
551007BV00004B/13/P